Learn Together

Junior Maths 1

Multiplication tables

Number patterns

Number stories

Tens and units

First fraction work

By
Sandra Soper

Illustrations by Suzanne Kemmenoe

A Piccolo Original
Piccolo Books

A note to parents

One of the most important aspects of this book will be the conversation it will stimulate as you work through the pages together.

The age range suggested on the cover is only approximate and you should not take it as a rigid guideline. Children develop at different rates and if the work proves difficult for the child, give as much help in the way of concrete materials as necessary. Talk about the work on each page before the child writes anything, so that you can discover the level of understanding and give the right kind of help. Gradually build on this level of understanding, adapting the ideas in this book and adding those of your own. Never rush a child on to a stage before he is ready, this will only confuse him. We hope that this book will help the child enjoy maths, so don't turn the work into a chore. Keep the sessions reasonably short and praise effort whenever you can.

We also hope that this book will form a link between home and school, so find out what the handwriting and number policies are at the child's school and use the work here to support these policies.

Children enjoy the sense of achievement felt on finishing a task, so after each activity there is a box which the child can tick if the work has been completed satisfactorily. It is important to avoid a sense of failure, so if a mistake is made, don't make a fuss about it. Use the opportunity to ask the child how he reached the answer and encourage him to have another go.

The instructions are there for guidance only and don't need to be followed slavishly. Similarly, the extra suggestions are only starters and your own ideas will be equally valuable.

Finally and most importantly, the book should be part of an all-round experience and exploration of maths (in the kitchen, garden, supermarket, car or school). Remember too that the child will only gain the maximum benefit if the book is *enjoyed*.

Those interested in the theory behind the maths covered in this book will find an explanation on the inside back cover. Also included in the book is a page of reward stickers with suggestions for their use.

Complete the 4+5 pattern up to 100.

1	2	3	④	5	6	7	8	⑨	10
11	12	13	⑭	15	16	17	18	⑲	20
21	22	23	㉔	25	26	27	28	㉙	30
31	32	33	34	35	36	37	38	39	40
41	42	43	44	45	46	47	48	49	50
51	52	53	54	55	56	57	58	59	60
61	62	63	64	65	66	67	68	69	70
71	72	73	74	75	76	77	78	79	80
81	82	83	84	85	86	87	88	89	90
91	92	93	94	95	96	97	98	99	100

"4 and 5 make"

The child rings the number 4 as shown, counts along 5, then rings the 9. Repeat this in each line and read the patterns aloud, stressing the pattern 4+5=9, 14+5=19, etc. These patterns are interesting for the child and learning them will save time and effort in later work. Experiment with different number bonds in different coloured felt pens, e.g. 2+6, 12+6, 22+6; 3+3, 13+3, 23+3, etc.

Martin worked hard. He did nineteen sums. Five were wrong and fourteen were right. Write a sum about this.

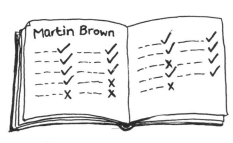

Ask the child to point to the sum in this story (14+5=19) on the number square above. Talk about how sums can be illustrated as stories to encourage the notion that sums 'mean' something beyond the numbers on the page. Make up some stories together – one partner makes up a story and the other spots the 'sum' and says it aloud, then vice versa.

Count the posts in the fence. How many?

When this fence was new there were 24 posts altogether. How many posts are missing now?

_____

Read the sum about the fence, then write it out in figures underneath.

Twenty-four minus five leaves nineteen

_____ ☐

> The idea at this stage is to help the child to relate his number work to his personal experience. Also to remember that numbers represent things in the physical world.

Use the number line to help you to take away from 24.

| 1 | 2 | 3 | 4 | 5 | 6 | 7 | 8 | 9 | 10 | 11 | 12 | 13 | 14 | 15 | 16 | 17 | 18 | 19 | 20 | 21 | 22 | 23 | 24 |

$24 - 3 =$ $24 - 24 =$

$24 - 4 =$ $24 - 20 =$

$24 - 5 =$ $24 - 21 =$ ☐

> Make two number strips as shown  to demonstrate these sums. So that for 24−3 the child can see that 21 is left, therefore 24−3=21. Point out that 24−3=21 is a variation of 4−3=1.

Read the number stories aloud before you answer the questions.

What is the total number of pencils in a box in which there are four green, six black and five orange pencils?

_____

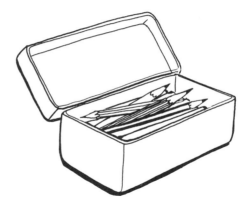

> Talk about the kind of sum needed to solve these stories, i.e. addition or subtraction, before the child works out the answer.

Twelve goldfish were taken from a fish tank to be sold at the fair. This left eighteen fish in the tank. How many fish were there to start with?

_____

Fourteen children from a class of twenty eight children went out of the classroom to see the school nurse. How many children were left in the classroom?

_____

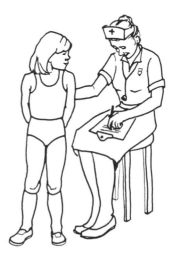

> Explain that the child should write words as well as numbers in the answer, e.g. 18 pencils/30 goldfish, etc.

3

Complete the number chain, then read it aloud.

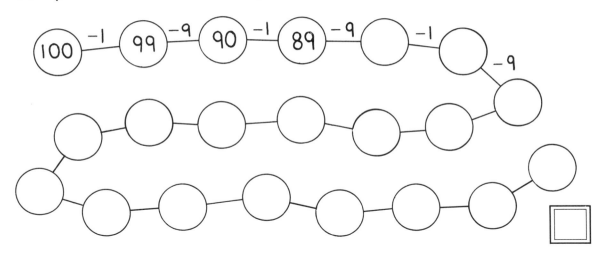

> The child could colour the pattern by circling all the 'tens' in one colour, all the 'nines' in a different colour. Make up more chains using different number bonds of ten: 7/3, 6/4, 2/8, etc. This helps to reinforce the early number bonds while also applying them to higher numbers.

Which child shows the highest score? _____

By how much is Neil's score more than Sue's? _____

Whose score is nearest to Amy's? _____

> Explain, if necessary, that each child's score is the total of the two numbers shown.

Go over the even numbers, then count them aloud to twenty.

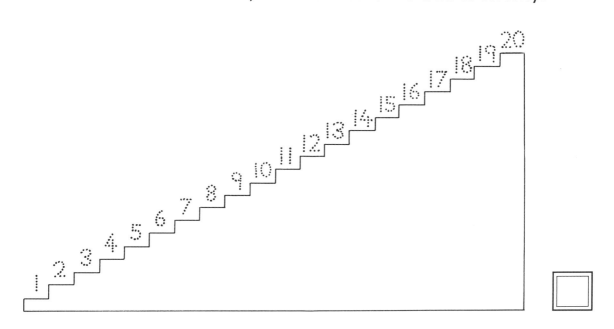

Score out the price on the ticket and write down half the price beside it.

Halving something is the same as dividing it by 2. Play question and answer games on halving. Take it in turns to ask the questions. Vary the format, half of 20, 100 divided by 2, etc.

5

Write the missing numbers, then read the table aloud.

2 × 1 =
 × 2 = 4
2 × 3 =
2 × 4 =
 × 5 =
2 ×   = 12
2 × 7 =
2 × 8 =
2 ×   = 18
2 × 10 =

Colour every second bead.

It is important that the child understands how the table is made, i.e.
2×1 oo , 2×2 oo oo , 2×3 oo oo oo
(use conkers, buttons, etc. to show the table in 3D). It is also important that the tables are learnt by heart so that they can be used with speed and ease in later work. There are two ways of organising tables and various ways of saying them out loud: 2×1=2 or 1×2=2
 2×2=4   2×2=4
 2×3=6   3×2=6
While the child is learning the tables, their presentation should be consistent, so check with the school and use that presentation.

Read the cost of each item aloud.

lollipop   22p

drink   cake

What would be the cost of

2 bars of chocolate?   2 cakes?

2 cans of drink?   2 lollipops?

6

Can you divide the marbles equally between Mark and Neil?

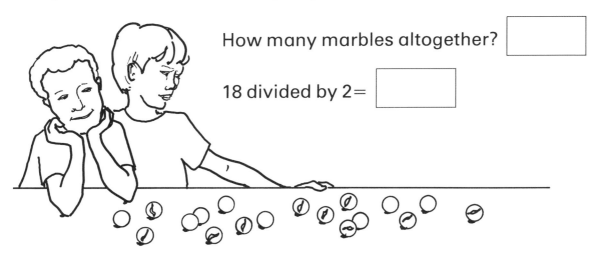

How many marbles altogether? ☐

18 divided by 2 = ☐

How many marbles will each boy have? Write your answer in a sentence.

_____ ☐

Let the child use actual objects if necessary and play around with groupings to show that, for example, 2×9=9×2

Divide by 2. ☐

4 ⟶ ☐	12 ⟶ ☐
6 ⟶ ☐	14 ⟶ ☐
8 ⟶ ☐	16 ⟶ ☐
10 ⟶ ☐	18 ⟶ ☐

Use a variety of materials and methods (buttons, number lines, etc.) to help the child and to add intertest and enjoyment.

7

Use the number line to help you to answer the questions.

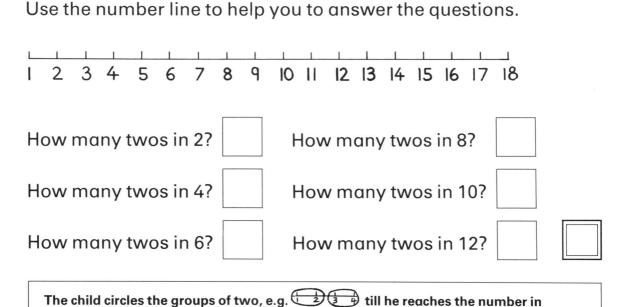

How many twos in 2? ☐   How many twos in 8? ☐

How many twos in 4? ☐   How many twos in 10? ☐

How many twos in 6? ☐   How many twos in 12? ☐   ☐

> The child circles the groups of two, e.g. ①② ③④ till he reaches the number in question. Play the game orally first before the child writes the answers. Ask each other more questions like this and keep a score sheet to add to the fun.

Colour every second square to make the pattern of the two times table.

1	2	3	4	5	6	7	8	9	10
11	12	13	14	15	16	17	18	19	20
21	22	23	24	25	26	27	28	29	30
31	32	33	34	35	36	37	38	39	40
41	42	43	44	45	46	47	48	49	50
51	52	53	54	55	56	57	58	59	60
61	62	63	64	65	66	67	68	69	70
71	72	73	74	75	76	77	78	79	80
81	82	83	84	85	86	87	88	89	90
91	92	93	94	95	96	97	98	99	100

☐

> Use egg trays to make large 100 squares. Marbles, sweets, milk tops, etc. can be used to mark out number patterns.

Read the number stories aloud together before you answer the questions.

Five children each bought two rubbers. How many rubbers is this altogether?

_____

Simon had £3 in his money box. Lisa had two times as much as this. How much money did Lisa have?

_____

When they were playing, David divided 14 beads equally between his 2 sisters. How many beads did each girl have?

_____

As before talk about the kind of sum required to work out these stories, and make up some more for each other to solve.

Mark the new price on each label.

Take ten from

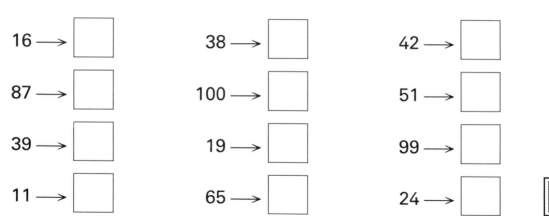

16 →
87 →
39 →
11 →

38 →
100 →
19 →
65 →

42 →
51 →
99 →
24 →

Write words for the answers.

Eighteen take away seven is _____

Twenty minus four is _____

Thirty minus twenty is _____

Ninety minus ten is _____

Forty-five less five is _____

> Read the sums aloud first and note how the child works out the answers.

Find the difference.

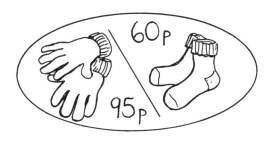

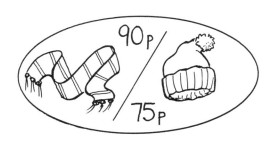

> Explain that the child should write the word 'difference' after the amount in the answer line, e.g. 10p difference.

11

Use the number line to help you answer the sums below.

21 22 23 24 25 26 27 28 29 30 31 32 33 34 35 36 37 38 39 40 41 42 43 44 45 46 47 48 49 50 51 52 53 54 55

26cm − 5cm = ☐   28cm − 5cm = ☐

30cm − 5cm = ☐   55cm − 5cm = ☐

48cm − 5cm = ☐   42cm − 5cm = ☐

51cm − 5cm = ☐   33cm − 5cm = ☐ ☐

> You could make paper ribbons to the lengths here and let the child actually cut off the required length and say the sums orally before they are recorded. Remind the child to include cm in the answer (and explain what this means if necessary).

Read these sums and answer them aloud before filling in the answer.

```
  26        35        39        28
 − 5       − 5       − 5       − 5
 ———       ———       ———       ———

  16        19        11        18
 − 5       − 5       − 5       − 5
 ———       ———       ———       ———
```

☐

> It is important for the child to do these sums mentally first. The writing part of this activity is to practise setting out sums and they are not intended to involve 'carrying'. Make sure the figures in the answer are in the correct columns.

12

Can you do these sums and then read them forwards and backwards?

Count each row of marbles, then put the total in the triangle. Now colour 3 marbles, then write the sum.

3 + 10 = 13

Read the sum forwards and backwards.

Colour 8 marbles, then write the sum.

☐ + ☐ = △

Colour 5 marbles, then write the sum.

☐ + ☐ = △

Colour 11 marbles, then write the sum.

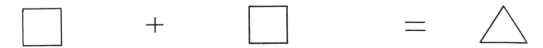

☐ + ☐ = △

The child counts the whole row of marbles, then writes the total in the triangle. Next the child colours the given number of marbles, writes the sum, then reads it forwards, 3+10=13, and backwards, 13=10+3.

13

Can you make the scales balance?

4+8 △ 8+☐   9+6 △ 6+☐   7+6 △ 6+☐
  /12\   /15\   /13\

9+8 △ 8+☐   3+11 △ 11+☐ 10+9 △ 9+☐
  /17\   /14\   /19\

> Embedded in every number fact there are three others, e.g. 3+4=7, 4+3=7, 7−4=3, 7−3=4. Help the child to see this and use a variety of concrete material to help if necessary.

Read the sums along and down. Complete all the boxes.

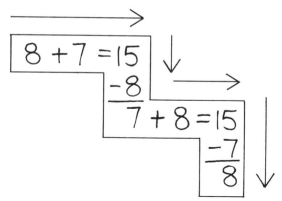

> Read the sum, '8 and 7 make 15, 15 minus 8 is 7, 7 and 8 make 15, 15 minus 7 is 8'.

The reward stickers
As an added incentive, we have included a sheet of reward stickers. Either reward the child for a special effort, or let him choose his ten best pages of work to put the sticker on.

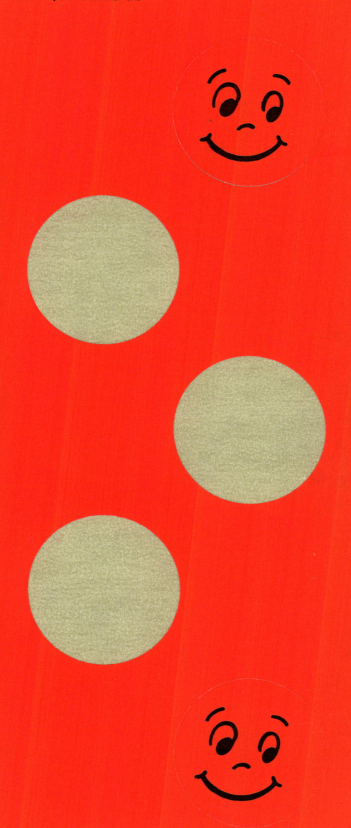

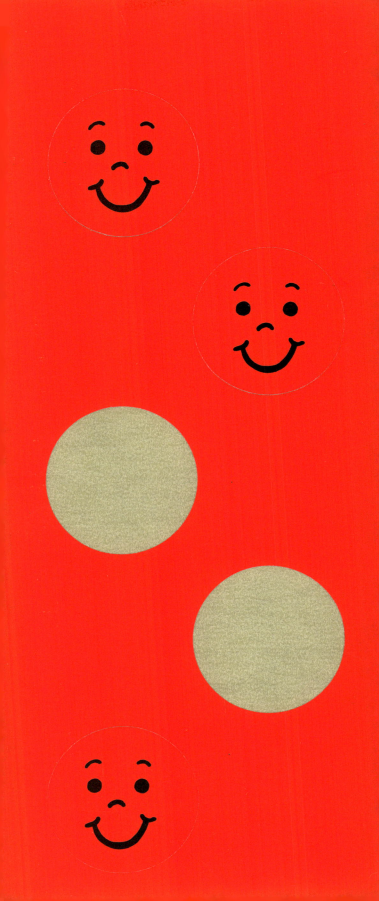

Write the answers in the boxes.

△
How many triangles? ☐   △ △
                        How many triangles? ☐

How many sides? ☐   How many sides? ☐

△ △ △
How many triangles? ☐   △ △ △ △
                        How many triangles? ☐

How many sides? ☐   How many sides? ☐

> Draw, colour and cut out triangles to use in tables games. Ask, 'How many sides are there in 6 triangles?/How many triangles can be made from 18 sides?' etc.

Colour every third box to give the pattern of the three times table. Read the coloured numbers aloud.

1	2	3	4	5	6	7	8	9	10
11	12	13	14	15	16	17	18	19	20
21	22	23	24	25	26	27	28	29	30
31	32	33	34	35	36	37	38	39	40
41	42	43	44	45	46	47	48	49	50
51	52	53	54	55	56	57	58	59	60
61	62	63	64	65	66	67	68	69	70
71	72	73	74	75	76	77	78	79	80
81	82	83	84	85	86	87	88	89	90
91	92	93	94	95	96	97	98	99	100

> Encourage the continuation of the pattern to 100. 'What do you think will happen to the pattern in the next row?'

Complete the three times table then read it aloud.

3 × 1 =
3 × 2 =
3 × 3 =
3 × 4 =
3 × 5 =
3 × 6 =
3 × 7 =
3 × 8 =
3 × 9 =
3 × 10 =

Colour every third triangle.

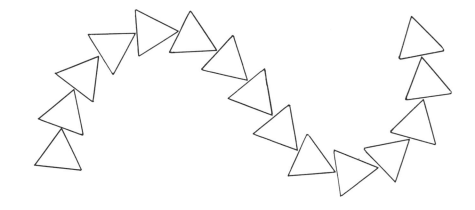

Again the child should be helped to learn the table by heart. Play question and answer games at odd moments to help him to memorise it.

Play the spiral game.

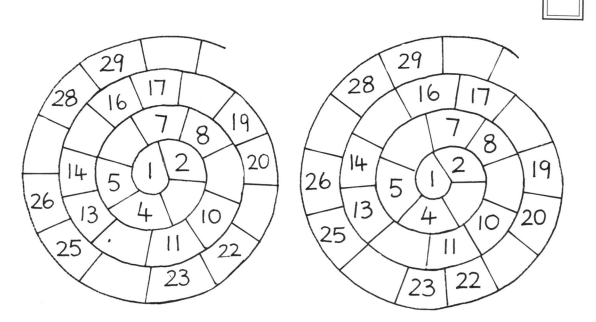

Choose a spiral. Write numbers 1–30 on scraps of paper and put them in an old margarine tub with a lid. Shake the box, remove the lid, then pick a number. If the number you pick is in the three times table, fill it in the spiral. First to complete the spiral wins. If the child is unsure of the table he can check his answers from the table above.

Write words in the answer boxes.

Three times what makes nine?

Three times six equals?

Thirty divided by three is?

How many threes in thirty?

> **Read these aloud first and talk about an alternative way of saying the sum, e.g. thirty divided by three, how many threes in thirty? etc. Let the child use counters, etc. if necessary and note his mental reasoning as the answer is worked out.**

Each girl is three times as old as her brother. Can you write the age of each girl?

James is 3 years old.

_____

Rajiv is 4 years old.

_____

Dan is 5 years old. His sister is

_____

> **Explain that the child should include the words 'years old' in the answer line.**

17

Read the number stories aloud before you write your answers.

When they came out of the fruit shop, Angela gave 3 plums to each of her 4 friends. How many plums is this altogether?

_____

John has invited 6 people to his party. He wants to give them each 3 balloons.
How many balloons must he buy?

_____

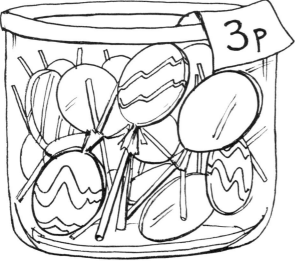

How many 3p lollipops could you buy for 30p?

_____

Remind the child to include words as well as figures in the answers.

Read the first line aloud, then complete the lines.

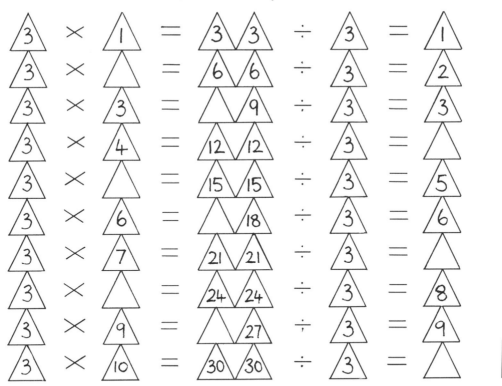

The reading aloud is important. Give the child as much help as necessary. Read alternate lines, or one read the multiplication side and one the division side, before the answers are filled in. When the table has been completed, point out that it could be read the other way round, e.g. first line 3×1=3 or 1×3=3. Remember to check with the school and use the same method.

Colour the numbers which can be divided exactly by three.

Explain and demonstrate if necessary that 'divided exactly' means with no remaining numbers left over.

19

How many tens in these numbers?

20 $\longrightarrow$ 2 tens

36 $\longrightarrow$ 3 tens

42 $\longrightarrow$

49 $\longrightarrow$

57 $\longrightarrow$

50 $\longrightarrow$

39 $\longrightarrow$

19 $\longrightarrow$

66 $\longrightarrow$

11 $\longrightarrow$

How many units?

16 $\longrightarrow$ 6 units

72 $\longrightarrow$ 2 units

90 $\longrightarrow$

88 $\longrightarrow$

10 $\longrightarrow$

100 $\longrightarrow$

The idea of this activity is to prepare the child for 'carrying' in tens and units. There should be a sound understanding of what, for example, 4 tens and 6 units means, before any attempt is made at carrying sums.

Write the numbers.

3 tens and 2 units ⟶ ◯   6 tens and 6 units ⟶ ◯

5 tens and 0 units ⟶ ◯   1 ten and 1 unit ⟶ ◯

6 tens and 4 units ⟶ ◯   4 tens and 8 units ⟶ ◯

7 tens and 9 units ⟶ ◯   8 tens and 0 units ⟶ ◯

2 tens and 2 units ⟶ ◯   9 tens and 5 units ⟶ ◯

Do some of these orally first to test the child's understanding fully.

Draw the numbers on the tens and units chart.

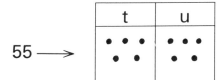

55 ⟶ [t: ••••• / u: •••••]   82 ⟶ [ ]

24 ⟶ [ ]   19 ⟶ [ ]

67 ⟶ [ ]   91 ⟶ [ ]

21

Draw the beads on the tens and units strings, then add two more beads. Draw and write the new total.

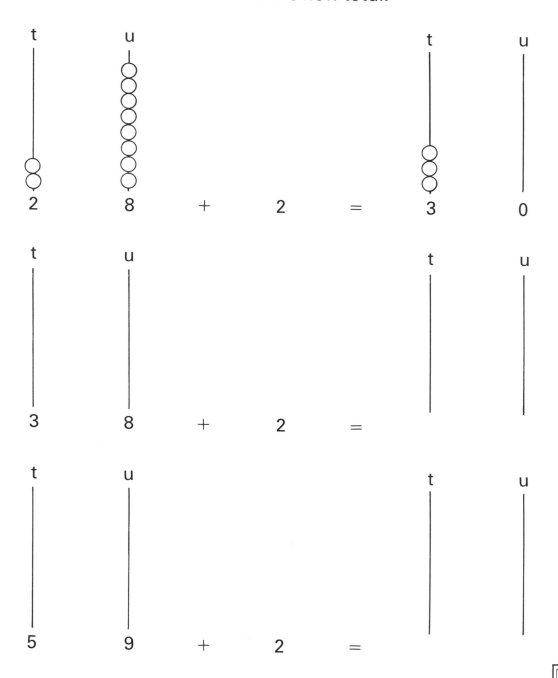

Here ten units beads must be changed for one ten bead. Don't force the child to draw beads if he doesn't need to. This is an introduction to place value which often needs a lot of practice. Note the child's working and mental reasoning, listen to his explanations and discuss them if necessary.

Can you total the points for each child?

> If necessary ask the child to work out aloud so that you can note his mental reasoning, and clear up any misunderstandings.

Read the words aloud, then write a sentence for your answer.

Jane won three points, then six points, then seven points. What was the total number of Jane's points?

_____

> Encourage the child to write out the calculations in the form of a sum if this helps and talk about what would be a suitable sentence before the child writes it.

Can you do these sums? Remember to start at the units side.

t. u.	t. u.	t. u.	t. u.
2 6	3 2	6 6	4 5
+ 4	+ 8	+ 6	+ 5

t. u.	t. u.	t. u.	t. u.
1 9	1 1	7 7	8 4
+ 2	+ 9	+ 3	+ 7

Find out how the child's school deals with carrying and follow the school so that the child is not confused by conflicting methods.

Use the 100 square to check your answers to the sums above.

1	2	3	4	5	6	7	8	9	10
11	12	13	14	15	16	17	18	19	20
21	22	23	24	25	26	27	28	29	30
31	32	33	34	35	36	37	38	39	40
41	42	43	44	45	46	47	48	49	50
51	52	53	54	55	56	57	58	59	60
61	62	63	64	65	66	67	68	69	70
71	72	73	74	75	76	77	78	79	80
81	82	83	84	85	86	87	88	89	90
91	92	93	94	95	96	97	98	99	100

24

Use the number lines to help you to add and subtract.

Add 3
→

| | | | | | | | | | | | | | | | | | | | |
11 12 13 14 15 16 17 18 19 20 21 22 23 24 25 26 27 28 29 30

11+3=☐   18+3=☐   20+3=☐   27+3=☐

Take 3
←

19 20 21 22 23 24 25 26 27 28 29 30 31 32 33

24−3=☐   26−3=☐   22−3=☐   31−3=☐

Add 4
→

36 37 38 39 40 41 42 43 44 45 46 47 48 49 50 51 52 53 54

37+4=☐   39+4=☐   40+4=☐   46+4=☐

Take 4
←

50 51 52 53 54 55 56 57 58 59 60 61 62 63 64 65 66 67 68 69

69−4=☐   63−4=☐   61−4=☐   68−4=☐

The child can write on the number line 20 21 22 23 to help to find the answer.
See how many sums you can make up in 2/3/4 minutes. Draw different number lines to give a wide variety of practice.

Increase each price by 5p.

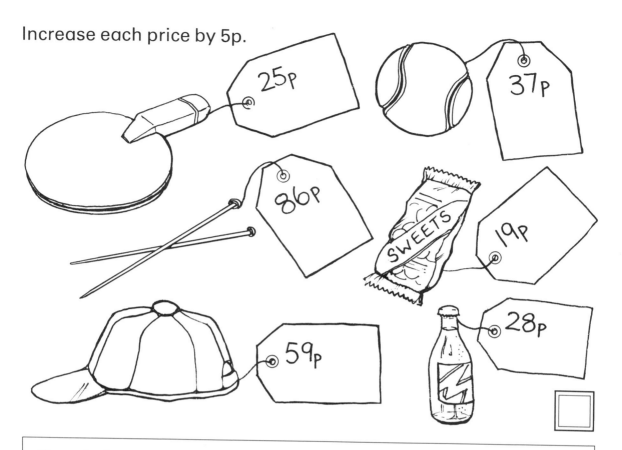

Note whether the child is still counting on in ones, and if so draw attention to the patterns in addition like those on page 1. Devise some practice sums like those below to help child to remember the patterns.

Can you do these sums?

9+3=	10−7=	5+6=
19+3=	20−7=	15+6=
29+3=	30−7=	25+6=
39+3=	40−7=	35+6=
49+3=	50−7=	45+6=

These can be done with the aid of a hundred square to show the child the spatial pattern as well as the numerical one.

Read the number stories aloud before you work out the answers.
Remember to write a word as well as a number in your answers.

The toy aeroplane costs 90p.
The toy boat costs 40p.
What is the difference in
price between the two?

Peter was 7 years old.
His brother was 4 years older
than this. How old was Peter's
brother?

Mary collected 17 conkers.
Kate collected 24 conkers.
How many conkers did the
girls have between them?

Colour *half* of each shape. The sign for half is ½. Write this sign on the coloured part of each shape.

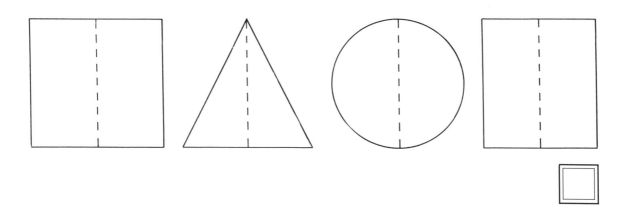

> Do not worry the child unnecessarily about the mathematical meaning of the sign ½. If it is of interest to the child you can explain that the sign means:
> 1 part of something which has been divided by 2
> similarly ⅓ means 1 part of something which has been divided by 3
> and ¼ means 1 part of something which has been divided by 4
> whereas ¾ means 3 parts of something which has been divided by 4.
> Make more shapes like those above to try different ways of halving each shape.

Write half of each number.

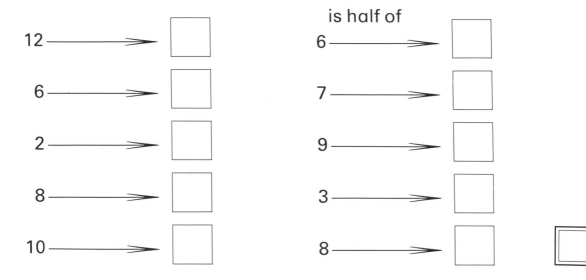

> The child should have lots of practice with 'real' halves — halving string, ribbon, cakes, apples, amounts of marbles, sweets, water, sand, etc. before meeting formal fractions on paper.

Read the number stories aloud before you work out the answer.

At the party Mashood filled a litre jug with lemonade. He poured half of the lemonade into some paper cups. How much lemonade was left in the jug?

Anne cut 2 metres of rope in half to make 2 skipping ropes.
What length was each skipping rope?

Sara's piano lesson lasted for 30 minutes. David's lesson lasted half as long. For how many minutes did David's lesson last?

If the child seems at all perplexed by these problems, then do the activity. Sometimes it is the formal wording which hinders understanding so, in this case, use lemonade, rope and a clock to link the activity to the words which describe it.

Read these sums aloud, then complete the four sums in the
other boxes.

7+5=12
5+7=12
12−7= 5
12−5= 7

7	6	13	13
+6	+7	−6	−7
13	13	7	6

10+7=17
7
17
17

12	2	14	14
+2			
14			

11+8=19
8
19
19

14			
+6			
20			

Ask the child to choose one of these sums and make up a number story about it. You
guess, then tick the chosen sum.